Seasons of the Tallgrass Prairie

written and illustrated by

CAROL LERNER

William Morrow and Company
New York 1980

Printed in the United States of America.
1 2 3 4 5 6 7 8 9 10

Library of Congress Cataloging in Publication Data

Lerner, Carol.
  Seasons of the tallgrass prairie.
  Summary: Describes the plant life of the American prairie,
season by season, and the role of wildfire in its ecology.
  1. Prairie flora–Juvenile literature. 2. Seasons–Juvenile literature.
3. Prairie flora–Middle West–Juvenile literature. 4. Seasons–Middle West–
Juvenile literature. 5. Fire ecology–Middle West–Juvenile literature.
[1. Prairie plants. 2. Fire ecology. 3. Ecology] I. Title. II. Title:
Tallgrass prairie.
QK938.P7L47   581.5'2643'0977   80-13078
ISBN 0-688-22245-5   ISBN 0-688-32245-X (lib. bdg.)

By the Same Author
On the Forest Edge
Flowers of a Woodland Spring

title page: bobolink, purple coneflowers, compass plant leaf
opposite: blue-eyed grass, Indian paintbrush

CONTENTS

In memory of Marlie Moulton

The Landscape

Step onto the narrow path that leads through the summer prairie. The tallgrasses, only half-grown, are hip high now, and the ground seems to rise and tumble as the rich mass of green blades obeys the movements of the wind. When the grasses bend to the breeze, long waves of shadow chase across the field.

The only sound on all the vast grassland is the murmur of plant against plant as the wind ruffles the thick, low growth. Only a few dark shapes stand without moving on the sea of swaying grasses– here and there the sturdy forms of bur oak trees, and far off a line of willow trees marking the place where a shallow stream bed cracks the smooth plains. The same green sea stretches in all directions as far as the skyline–flat, unbroken, monotonous.

But look more closely among the grasses around your feet. Blossoms of orange and pink and white are scattered all through the tangle of grasses, blazes of color against the cool green. Stretching your arms, you can almost touch a dozen different kinds of bright flowers. Some of them stand alone–a single flower or two, different from all those surrounding it. Others blossom among a whole crowd of their own kind in a cheerful cluster. It is not an orderly flower bed, but it is a rich one.

These are not the plants of our vacant lots and country roadsides. Pale-blue chicory and the cheerful daisies and dandelions do not belong in this landscape. Many of the familiar weeds of today's waste places did not grow in this country until they were brought here from the old world and spread by the pioneers.

mountain mint

wild quinine

prairie lily

tall green milkweed

prairie coreopsis

thimbleweed

All of these prairie plants, filling the fields to the skyline, are native Americans. They are the plants that the Indians knew and used. They greeted the American pioneer when the first immigrant wagon cut ruts into the grassy carpet. Reaching western Indiana, the pioneers stepped out of the familiar gloom of the Eastern forests into the blinding sunshine of Midwestern prairie. The landscape was different from anything they had ever seen.

Soon the steel plow was turning under the long ribbons of prairie earth, heavy with its dense cover of growing plants, and making the prairie into some of the best farmland in the world. Large fields planted with a single crop took the place of the patchwork prairie plant community. The native plant life on most of the original American prairie was soon destroyed by farming and by grazing.

Even in the prairie heartland, most people today have never seen a piece of American prairie. But though only a few states still contain large pieces of native grassland, most of the original prairie states have some small patches, prairie remnants, that have survived by chance. These remnants are part of the country's living history. They tell something about the special character of the prairie landscape, its rhythms and its beauty.

Usually the most common plants in a piece of prairie belong to the grass family. Though they are flowering plants, their flowers are too small to catch the eye. Only a few different kinds of grasses grow in one particular prairie–perhaps eight or ten at most. In wet places, the grasslike sedges may be the most numerous plants.

Yet there could be over a hundred different kinds of plants growing on a few acres of rich prairie. Most of them are forbs, the wild flowers of the prairie. The forbs bring color and change to the solid green of the grass fields.

Most forbs bloom for only a few weeks at one particular time in the season. Each week ten or twenty forbs may start to blossom. So the prairie puts on its own garden show, with the main display of flowers changing constantly. The only way to see all these hundred and more forbs in bloom is to visit the prairie every few weeks, all through the months of the growing season.

yellow star grass

above: valerian
below: prairie violet

violet wood sorrel

blue-eyed grass

Spring

Spring comes late to the prairie. In April, the fields still look dry and lifeless. The earth is piled with heaps of dead grasses and plant stems, lying where they fell last winter. The litter of dead plants is harsh to the touch. It crackles when you walk through it, and the strands of tough, brown grasses catch at your feet. Sharp young blades of grass are barely poking through the blanket of dead plants.

Bees hum over the flowers that are already open. Most of these blossoms are on low plants that hug the ground for protection. There are prairie violets and the violet wood sorrel. The yellow star grass, with leaves like blades of grass, dapples the earth with small, bright blossoms. Only the awkward stalk of the valerian stands high above the ground, far taller than the other flowers of the young season.

Many kinds of green leaves are pushing above the brown litter. Some are sharp and stiff. Others are soft and pale, covered with downy hairs. They are the early growth of the forbs and grasses that soon will spread over the prairie. But to understand the prairie, and the explosion of plant growth that is about to burst forth, you have to know something about what is under the blanket of dead plants, down in the prairie earth.

The soil is not crammed with sprouting seeds that will make up the year's growth. Instead, the earth is filled with old plant growth from the years before. Tough rhizomes trail off from the bottom of the grass plants, a few inches below the surface of the ground. They hold surplus food that the green parts of the plants have made. During dry summers, when the plants are unable to make much new food, the stored food is used to keep the plant alive and growing. When the rainfall is good, shoots grow up from the rhizomes to make more grasses. Over the long winter, the rhizomes hold the food for next spring's growth.

The grasses, and almost all of the prairie plants, are perennials. That is, each year's plants grow from the same underground parts;

only the parts aboveground die at the end of the growing season.

The storage bodies of the forbs–more rhizomes, and other underground stem parts called bulbs, corms, and tubers–are mixed in with the rhizomes and roots of the grass plants. Some of these underground parts stay alive and make new growth each year for twenty or fifty years or more. So the plants of the prairie may be as old as some of the large trees in the forest!

The top few inches of soil are filled with this tangled growth. Twisted and crammed together–roots, rhizomes, and the rest–they make a thick layer of tough fibers that hold the earth tightly. Blocks of this dense sod, cut from the surface of the prairie, were used to make the sod houses of the prairie pioneers.

Usually the larger part of a prairie plant is what lives underground, and the smaller part is what grows above. Because water is often scarce during the growing season, most of the prairie species send their roots far and deep into the soil to get enough moisture. With the water, they also take in dissolved minerals that they need for healthy growth. Often the roots of forbs go down ten feet or more, and some are over twenty feet deep.

When the plant finally dies, these far-reaching root systems decay and become humus–a dark black material. Humus loosens the texture of the soil and enables new roots to grow more freely. The humus has the ability to hold gases and large amounts of water. The rotted root systems hold these materials deep in the soil where other plants can use them.

A few prairie plants, such as the prairie violets, have very shallow root systems, which grow entirely in the top foot or two of the soil. A larger number of species have the greatest part of their root development in the layer of earth between two and five feet deep. But many send roots down more than five feet and take very little moisture from the upper two or three feet of soil. Sharing the soil in this way–different species putting out their greatest root development at different depths–many plants are able to grow together in a small space. Often 200 to 250 individual plants grow in a single square yard of earth.

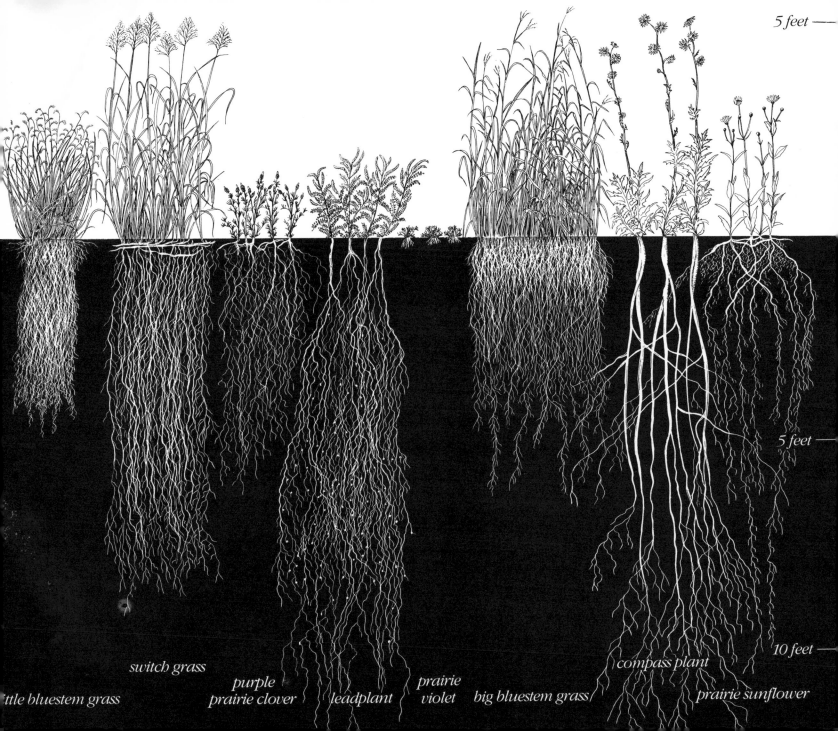

5 feet

5 feet

10 feet

switch grass

purple
prairie clover

leadplant

prairie
violet

big bluestem grass

compass plant

little bluestem grass

prairie sunflower

With so many perennial plants packed closely together, there is little opportunity for a new plant to get a foothold. A seed needs some space in the ground to send down a root. It needs water and must grow quickly enough so that it will not be shaded out by the other plants.

But the older plants need less space to start new growth. They can send up shoots from underground stem parts. Most plant growth on the prairie begins this way–from the underground parts of the old plants and not from seeds. As long as the underground plant parts stay alive, the prairie is a closed community.

By late May the grasses grow thickly enough to color the fields with fresh green and to hide the meadowlark's nest from sight. Now the prairie glows with the colors of the spring-blooming forbs. This display is the first in a series of changing flower shows that will unfold over the weeks to come.

The yellows and pinks catch the eye first. Brightest of all is the sulphur-yellow of the hoary puccoon. The plants are small, but clustered together and covered with flowers. The rich pink of prairie phlox adds the other strong note of color against the green background. Except for the golden Alexanders, most of the other flowers are softer in color and less bold. The forms of their flowers are delicate and varied. Their leaves make complicated patterns among the stiff, straight lines of the grass blades.

Most of these plants stand taller than the ones that flowered a month ago. The flowers now are at or above the tips of the grasses. As the season advances and the grasses lengthen, the forbs that are flowering will generally be taller and taller. A few of the ground huggers can still be seen through the grasses–the last of the prairie violets and bright white flowers of the wild strawberry. But these low plants are being shaded from the sunshine.

hoary puccoon

wild strawberry

golden Alexander

shooting star

prairie phlox   *prairie smoke*   *wild hyacinth*   *bluets*

One plant stands out for its larger size and thick bushy shape. It is called the cream wild indigo, with smooth, pale blossoms arching from the mass of leaves. Like most members of the pea family, it has small growths, or nodules, attached to its roots. The growths are caused by bacteria that enter the root and feed upon the plant. Inside the nodules, the bacteria take in nitrogen from the atmosphere and change it into a form that the plants can use. The bacteria do not harm the plant, and they provide a mineral that the plant needs for healthy growth.

When the plant dies and its roots rot, the useful nitrogen still in its tissues will become part of the prairie soil. Then the other prairie plants will be able to use the nitrogen for their growth. In this way, the forbs in the pea family enrich the soil where they grow. They are one of the largest groups of plants found on the prairie, in numbers of plants and in numbers of species. At least one of them can usually be found in flower at any time, from spring to fall.

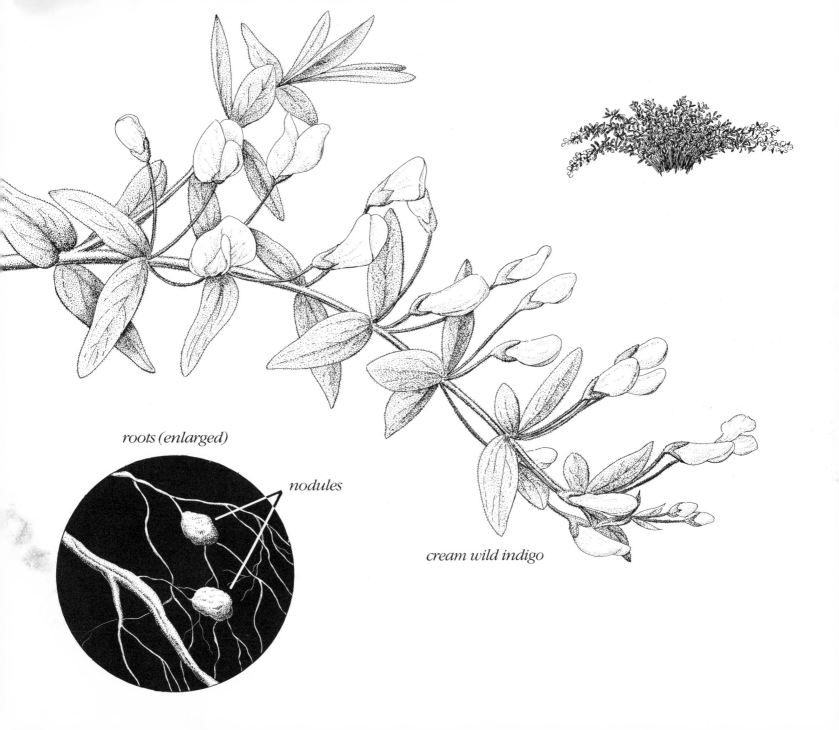

roots (enlarged)

nodules

cream wild indigo

Summer

Summer is a time of fulfillment on the prairie. It is the season that seems to suit it best. The sun is high; days are hot and long. But under the blistering sun, the prairie is lush and green. An army of insects feeds in the field, hidden by the cover of the grasses. At each step, grasshoppers explode from underfoot.

To walk across the prairie now is like wading through a rising sea, surrounded by tumbling waves of grass. Leaves of the compass plant–deeply cut, always standing with their edges pointing to the north and south–give some direction on this green ocean.

Spires of Culver's root hold their flowers in gentle curves, and rigid stalks of rattlesnake master push knobs of white blossoms above the grass tops. Other summer forbs supply a rainbow of color: pale yellow coneflowers, the glowing orange clusters of butterfly weed.

Culver's root

purple prairie clover   *compass plant leaf*   *prairie blazing star*   *yellow coneflower*

compass plant

butterfly weed

above: rattlesnake master

prairie dock leaf

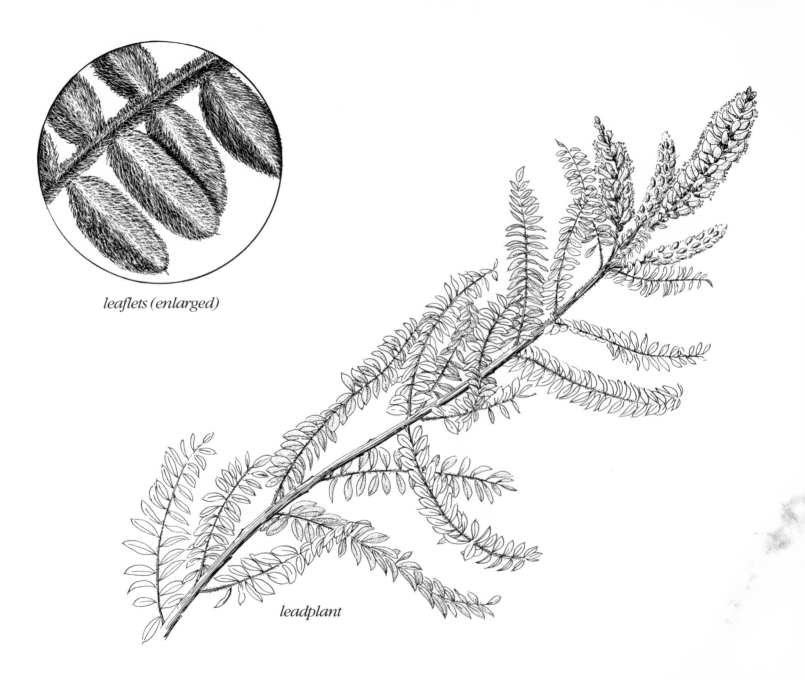

leaflets (enlarged)

leadplant

Few bushes grow on the prairie, so they stand out. One of them, the leadplant, is in flower now, and its spikes of purple and yellow flowers are brilliant when seen closely. From a distance, the plants look like gray-green heaps huddling on the prairie. Fine short hairs cover their leaves densely and give them a dull silvery color.

Many of the other prairie plants also have stems and leaves that are hairy or covered with fuzz. The hairs help to keep the plant from drying up by trapping the moisture that evaporates from it. This kind of structure is one of the adaptations to a dry climate.

Because there are few trees to shade the ground, and because the wind sweeps unchecked across the prairie plains, there is more evaporation on the prairie than in the forest. Periods without rainfall during the growing season are frequently a part of the weather pattern in prairie regions. Prairie plants have forms and growth habits that conserve moisture.

Some have thick leaves, and less water evaporates from thick leaves than from thin ones. Some have leaves that curl up or fold down the middle, so less surface is exposed to the sun and wind. Others have thick, sticky plant juices that hold the water and keep it from evaporating quickly.

The crowded way that plants grow gives some protection too. Taller plants shade the shorter ones, and they shade their own lower leaves. The air at ground level is much moister and cooler than the air above. The earth also protects the underground parts of plants from quick loss of water, and half or more of most of these plants is underground.

Just as the earth protects the plants, the growing plants protect the earth. Most rainfall in this region falls during the growing season, often in quick, heavy downpours. Raindrops beat upon the grasses and other leaves, but few hit bare ground.

Much of the rain that trickles down to the earth is held by the humus, like a great sponge. And the soil itself is held by the tangle of roots and underground stem parts. Erosion—the loss of topsoil from the forces of wind and water—is not a problem on the unbroken prairie. Very little soil is blown or washed away.

Through the bright weeks of the prairie summer, the grasses stretch taller and taller. The flowers of the early season are gone—prairie Indian plantain and leadplant have made their seeds and are hidden among the taller plants. Roundheaded bush clovers, sneezeweeds, and others take their place.

The grasses stand chest-high in many places, even taller than most of the late-summer forbs. But a few forbs–the prairie dock, tall coreopsis–still thrust their blossoms above the grass tops.

tall coreopsis

prairie dock

prairie sunflower

glaucous white lettuce

stiff goldenrod

New England aster

sky-blue aster

Fall

Fall brings a different look. The rainbow splash of colors is replaced by a few—yellow, purple, blue. The yellow is from masses of goldenrods and from the tall sunflower plants. Plants belonging to different species of the asters are scattered all over the field, and their colors range from the white heath aster, through all shades of blue, to the rich purple of the New England aster.

There may be six different kinds of asters and a dozen different goldenrods growing here. What they have in common is that all of them, and most of the forbs that flower in the fall, belong to the same huge composite family. They bloom at all times of the growing season, but in fall they dominate the fields.

Plants in the composite family take their family name from the arrangement of their flowers. What looks like a single, large sunflower blossom, or a single, small aster flower, is really many small flowers, or florets, arranged in a tightly packed head. Since it is a very large group, the details of the arrangement are different among the various family members. What they share is that their flowers *are* composite: that is, their heads are composed of many small florets.

Sunflowers and most asters have two kinds of florets in each head. The little tube-shaped structures crammed into the center are disk florets. The larger outer ones that look like petals are ray florets. Some of the other composites have a whole head made up only of disk florets, and others have only ray florets.

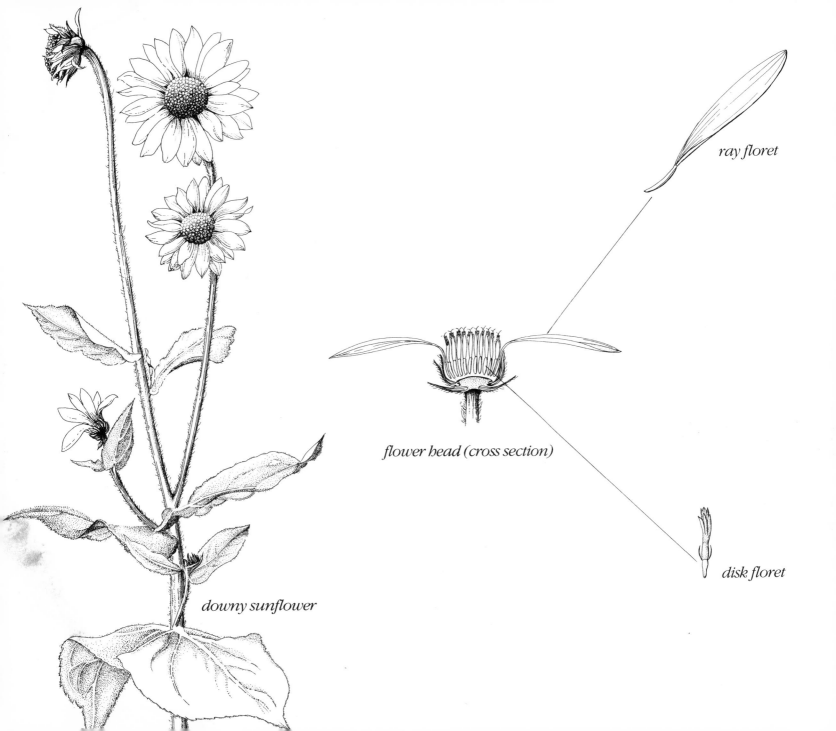

ray floret

flower head (cross section)

disk floret

downy sunflower

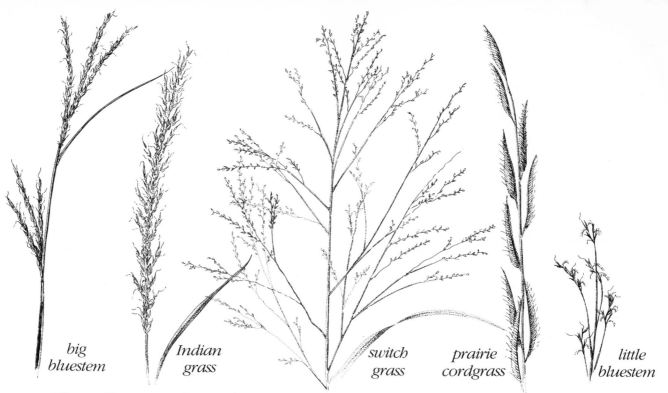

big bluestem *Indian grass* *switch grass* *prairie cordgrass* *little bluestem*

The tallgrasses have flowered too and are setting seeds, so now you can tell them apart easily. Big bluestem is sometimes called turkeyfoot grass because its seed clusters are often held in three branches, resembling the footprint of a turkey. Seeds of Indian grass are held densely, close to the stem, and switch grass has a graceful, loose spray. In wetter places, there are thick strands of prairie cordgrass with grass blades that have a cutting edge of small, sharp teeth. All of these grasses can grow six feet tall or more.

The little bluestem is only one to three feet tall, but it is common even on the tallgrass prairies. It grows in the drier places that are less suitable to the tallgrasses, and where it is not shaded from the sunlight by its taller relatives.

Among all the tall, thick growth, a few of the fall-flowering forbs must be searched out close to the ground. Here, at the bottom of the grasses, are the gentians. Their radiant blues, among the most intense of nature's colors, are the final splendors of the prairie season.

bottle gentian   *prairie gentian*

purple coneflower

above: switch grass

pasture thistle

roundheaded bush clover

By October the grasses have lost their green color. Now the prairie glows softly in shades of copper and tan. Most of the forbs have dried too and stand crisply in the fall breeze. Decorative seed heads are held stiffly among the pale grasses–the chocolate-brown of bush clover and the darker stalks of purple coneflower plants. Goldfinches teeter on the stiff stems of dried thistle plants, harvesting the seeds. Withered leaves and stems rustle in the wind.

There are just a few late-blooming asters and goldenrods in flower. The lowering sun shines through some flat, stiff leaves of the compass plant that still stand green and yellowing. Leathery, with the feel of sandpaper, they are among the last plants to give up to the season. Soon they will brown and wrinkle too, as the first frosts end another year's growth.

Winter

Winter comes to the prairie, and snow powders the limp piles of dead grasses. Dry plants stand like monuments–the stalks of compass plants, great leaves of prairie dock, handsome seed heads of the purple coneflowers. Their stiff forms sway and crackle as the wind pushes frozen air over the flat lands.

Now the prairie is a lonely place. The great hum and flutter of animal life that filled the prairie summer have stopped. The insects are underground or in the tissues of the plants, silent and unmoving. The summer birds have flown to warmer lands. Horned larks peck at stray seeds among the litter.

But down in the soil, the jumbled mass of bulbs and corms and rhizomes is protected from the bitter cold. Swift blizzards spread light blankets of snow over the earth that covers them. Beneath these layers, the prairie plants lie dormant, retaining life and storing food.

Fire

Trees grew in some places on the tallgrass prairie. Trees and shrubs bordered the streams and rivers that drained across the prairie lands. The settlers often came upon prairie groves–islands of sugar maples, ashes, and oaks–that gave welcome shade on the sunburned plain. Wherever prairie and woodland meet–on the edges of these groves and on the borders of the Eastern woodland–trees begin to spread into the grasslands.

Seeds from the trees and shrubs are scattered over the nearby prairie land. If they drop where there is space to take root, especially in years of plentiful rainfall, these seeds sprout and begin to grow. Slowly the forest invades the prairies.

As the trees and shrubs grow, they cast larger areas of shade over the ground. The prairie plants, adapted to live in full sunlight, grow poorly in these darker and cooler conditions. They become weaker and smaller, and finally they die out.

In the time of the Indians, fire checked the invading forest trees and kept the prairies open. After the growing season, when the stems and leaves of the prairie plants have dried, they are like tinder on the ground. A stray spark from a campfire is enough to start the flame. Indians commonly started prairie fires as an aid to hunting. The animals ran before the flames and were driven to places where they could be trapped and killed more easily.

The fire quickly becomes a tall sheet of flame, fanned by the wind and racing before it. Wherever the thick layer of dead plant material lies on the ground, it feeds the wall of flame. The fire even passes over the prairie marshes, burning the stalks of the dry sedges, grasses, and wetland forbs. Acres of dead plant leaves and stems are turned into black ashes in minutes.

The fire might roar across the plains for days. Finally a broad stream of water in its path, a change in the wind direction, or a sudden rainstorm stops it. There is almost nothing left afterward, except the black earth and the charcoal stumps of plants. Here and there, in low places, the flames have missed a spot, and a heap of dead stalks makes a patch of tan on the sooty field.

The prairie plants are not damaged by the sweep of fire. After the growing season, all of their living parts are down in the earth. But most of the young shrubs and trees that were growing on the prairie have been killed. In all seasons, they have a living layer of tissue under the bark. When fire streaks across the field, the parts of the woody plants that are aboveground are scorched or burned.

After the prairie lands were settled and fire no longer raged across unbroken fields, the prairie that remained began to fill with trees. Many of the Midwestern forests of today were still prairies at the time of pioneer settlement. Prairie remnants remain open only if the woody plants are kept out, either by fire or by cutting.

A few kinds of trees are able to survive the passage of the flames. The settlers often found clusters of small oak trees growing in the middle of the prairies. Though their growth was stunted by the frequent fires, these oaks were able to stay alive. The bur oak, especially, can survive even an intense prairie fire. It has a thick, corky bark, which is a layer of insulation, wrapping and protecting the living wood. After the fire, the bur oaks stand alone, rough figures with stiff, dark limbs sprawled on a sooty plain.

Just as fire keeps the prairie from becoming a forest, it also maintains the strength and variety of the prairie plants. On an unburned prairie, most of the dead plant materials on the ground at the end of the year will still be there next spring, and the following spring as well. The layer becomes thicker each year.

It begins to affect the growth of the prairie plants. It blocks the sunlight from shining on the earth. It insulates the ground from the warmer air of the springtime, so the soil keeps its winter cold for weeks longer. Plants begin growing later, and more slowly.

The more sensitive plants begin to weaken. The smaller forbs, those of early spring, are unable to thrust their way through the thick blanket of dead plant material. The more delicate species begin to die off. Unless the leftover material is removed, the great variety of plant life will be lost over the years.

The dead stalks and leaves contain many kinds of minerals taken from the soil. The far-reaching root systems of the prairie plants have mined the earth, bringing materials to the surface to become a part of the living plants. At the end of the season, a portion of these minerals lies useless on the ground, locked up in the dead parts of the plants.

Many of the plants have tough fibers and hard stems that rot very slowly. So years pass before the stems and leaves decay and the minerals return to the earth. But fire produces the change in an instant. Most of the minerals in the dead plant parts return to the soil with the ashes and can be used again for new growth.

Fire leaves the land looking desolate and bare. On this black plain, there is little that recalls the masses of flowers or the richness of plant and animal life that filled the land.

But the black earth will soak up the sun's warmth quickly, when pale spring sunshine spreads over the fields. Freed from the choking blanket of the dead plant materials and fed by the mineral-rich ashes, the plants in the soil will soon respond.

Young shoots will push through the charred earth and rise above the ashes of the old year. Leaves of all shapes and textures will unfold. Once again bright greens will color the ground, to signal the coming of another prairie spring.

Scientific Names
of Plants Mentioned or Illustrated in this Book

big bluestem grass
Andropogon gerardi
blue-eyed grass
Sisyrinchium albidum
bluets
Houstonia caerulea
bottle gentian
Gentiana andrewsii
bur oak
Quercus macrocarpa
butterfly weed
Asclepias tuberosa
compass plant
Silphium laciniatum
cream wild indigo
Baptisia leucophaea
Culver's root
Veronicastrum virginicum
downy sunflower
Helianthus mollis
glaucous white lettuce
Prenanthes racemosa
golden Alexander
Zizia aurea

heath aster
Aster ericoides
hoary puccoon
Lithospermum canescens
Indian grass
Sorghastrum nutans
Indian paintbrush
Castilleja coccinea
leadplant
Amorpha canescens
little bluestem grass
Andropogon scoparius
mountain mint
Pycnanthemum virginianum
New England aster
Aster novae-angliae
pasture thistle
Cirsium discolor
prairie blazing star
Liatris pycnostachya
prairie cordgrass
Spartina pectinata
prairie coreopsis
Coreopsis palmata

prairie dock
Silphium terebinthinaceum
prairie gentian
Gentiana puberula
prairie Indian plantain
Cacalia tuberosa
prairie lily
Lilium philadelphicum
prairie phlox
Phlox pilosa
prairie smoke
Geum triflorum
prairie sunflower
Helianthus laetiflorus
prairie violet
Viola pedatifida
purple coneflower
Echinacea pallida
purple prairie clover
Petalostemum purpureum
rattlesnake master
Eryngium yuccifolium
roundheaded bush clover
Lespedeza capitata
shooting star
Dodecatheon meadia
sky blue aster
Aster azureus

sneezeweed
Helenium autumnale
stiff goldenrod
Solidago rigida
switch grass
Panicum virgatum
tall coreopsis
Coreopsis tripteris
tall green milkweed
Asclepias hirtella
thimbleweed
Anemone cylindrica
valerian
Valeriana ciliata
violet wood sorrel
Oxalis violacea
wild hyacinth
Camassia scilloides
wild quinine
Parthenium integrifolium
wild strawberry
Fragaria virginiana
yellow coneflower
Ratibida pinnata
yellow star grass
Hypoxis hirsuta